WHEELS
AT WORK AND PLAY

ALL ABOUT

TRUCKS

For a free color catalog describing Gareth Stevens' list of high-quality children's books, call 1-800-341-3569 (USA) or 1-800-461-9120 (Canada).

Wheels at Work and Play
All about Diggers
All about Motorcycles
All about Race Cars
All about Special Engines
All about Tractors
All about Trucks

Library of Congress Cataloging-in-Publication Data

Stickland, Paul.
    All about trucks / Paul Stickland.
       p. cm. — (Wheels at work and play)
     Summary: Depicts a variety of trucks, including a builder's truck, tow truck, and tanker.
       ISBN 0-8368-0421-X
      1. Trucks—Juvenile literature. [1. Trucks.] I. Title. II. Series.
    TL230.15.S75   1990
    629.224—dc20   90-9819

This North American edition first published in 1990 by
Gareth Stevens Children's Books
1555 North RiverCenter Drive, Suite 201
Milwaukee, Wisconsin 53212, USA

First published in the United States in 1988 by Ideals Publishing Corporation with an original text copyright © 1986 by Mathew Price Ltd. Illustrations copyright © 1986 by Paul Stickland. Additional end matter copyright © 1990 by Gareth Stevens Inc.

Series editor: Tom Barnett
Designer: Laurie Shock

Printed in the United States of America

1 2 3 4 5 6 7 8 9 96 95 94 93 92 91 90

WHEELS
AT WORK AND PLAY

ALL ABOUT
TRUCKS

Paul Stickland

Gareth Stevens Children's Books
MILWAUKEE

The flatbed truck has a
flat bottom.

One truck carries a load.
One does not.

This is a builder's truck.
It has a special crane.

This crane loads and
unloads bricks.

This truck has broken down.

The tow truck pulls it to
a garage.

The tanker brings gasoline.

The red truck gets gas from the pump.

Container trucks hold goods.

They carry goods from
warehouses to stores.

These trees have been
cut down.

They will go to
the lumberyard.

Glossary

builder's truck
A truck that carries building tools and supplies.

container truck
A truck that carries goods long distances.

crane
A machine that lifts heavy objects.

flatbed
A flat trailer used to carry large objects.

lumberyard
A place where wood is cut and sold.

tanker
A truck that carries gasoline or other liquids.

tow truck
A strong truck that can pull other cars or trucks
when they need to be repaired.

warehouse
A building where goods are stored before they are delivered.

Index